THE KING OF BEAN

c Brent MacKay, 1981
ISBN 0-919626-16-5
Brick Books, Box 219
Ilderton, Ontario N0M 2A0

THE KING OF BEAN

Brent MacKay

Brick Books
Coldstream

Night's end thanks time
and tear of friends' embrace.

The day begins.

Raindrop
slides to tip
of vinemaple leaf,
strains release
of gathering weight
and falls followed
by another.

Veins of water
run together
a lace of life
to adorn growth
or death
the same morning.

Forest and garden glisten
in a rivermist
sitting on the valley.
Golden Ears ripens
in the gradual light
over Mission and Surrey;
Whistler and Garibaldi stir
as Grouse begins an outline
below the lions.

Atkinson blinks in the west
though birds are awake;
nets set for pinks and spring
shake on the winch;
the greenchain greets first light
at Port Moody.

Limbs ache,
trolleys lurch,
Broadway, Kingsway, Hastings
still asleep to the Wayne's
bristles sweeping the curb.

Delta men,
men of Tsawassen
and Lulu Island,
men in turbans,
men of China, Japan and Holland
collect vegetables
from earth black as tar.

Gangs from the barn
head for ship and shed
at Ballyntine, Centennial, C.P.R.

By eight, Cassiar's
backed-up to the Port Mann,
Portulo's a snarl;
Lion's Gate, Second Narrows,
Oak Street
come to a crawl.

At bus-stops,
umbrellas in hand,
girls blare between droplets
as rainfern frenchhorn
uncurls allgreen, wet;

fishbone-shape orchestrates
a morning triolet
to all the traffic.

Snails to stucco swirl,
unaware of the world.

II

Opening my closet
a kind season's pirouette
forgets dawn
with a sheen of light
steaming rooftop, sidewalk
and turnip tip.

Sails tack off Point Grey;
translucent dogwood
floats on a salt-scented wave;
foxglove and buttercup
respond to bee and heat
in lanes overgrown
with blackberry and poppy.

Offices empty seeking sun
onto Georgia and Burrard;
serrated mountains
become blue and green
with each fir discernible.

The afternoon verbs sportscars,
Scarlatti on a turntable;

jazz radio trumpet staccato
spinning in a paradise
of calendar abandon,
day to day seldom random,
seldom carpe diem
for a heart unable to blaze.

Lie links lie
as mackerel skies
offer alibis
to travel maps
on a fingertip.

Corner meets corner
to walls stretching
to the next corner;
turning left to shoulder more stone
or right to more loneliness
is all guesswork,
stepping stones directionless.

Logs line beaches
from Spanish Banks
to Ambleside;
languid hours
settle on lawns
from Kerrisdale
to Killarney
and Burnaby beyond.

Proud nipples point out
summer's full breast
as sprinklers arc spectrums
under an amber cloud
stretching from the inlet south.

Packed, ticket in order,
smelt nets shimmer
as a sunset more brilliant
than salmon spawning
describes mist descending
each trailing mountain
to a pale horizon.

It is the hour
sawdust barges lumber to anchor
hard-by freighters impatient for grain.

It is the hour
no words distill time
or transcribe ticking
in the nacre of waves;
in the redolent, relentless
wrestle on rock
to stretch from flesh
swirling on sea's havoc.

No twitch unlocks lyric;
no outline releaves blur of doubt.

Long after pavement looses heat
children melt in shadows
of hide and seek.

False Creek is still;
light goes by in ripples
while swallows dart
Sweeney's barrels.

Pacific gulls and clouds
glide in from the strait
on a west wind fanning yellow fumes
on the moon's face;
Venus follows more exotic on blue
than a jewel.

IV

And they will say
'The collywobbles got him;
his noggin prolapsed like collop
and he collapsed into thin air.'

The star is gone;
a spider slides
to support his web
from a hydrangea
on the boulevard.

Roses wilt, peaches drop
ripe from stems unseen;
skies knot with wind,
fishermen are drowned
in moonlight like wishbones on sea.

It is time to leave;
the song is spit
in a bird's throat.

Fool's blood fuels straw
disheartened on a loop
of youthful streets
to seek small sense.

From a thousand feet
Granville's ablaze
on a patchwork
of candle seams.

Not wept ripe
or rigid

a hand
resting
on a pelvis

without
thought
or control

like a bird
on a wall

melts
a pulse

of touch
weeping

sad moments
of flesh

fleeting
in a pigeon's
blink.

Not much more 13

this history
of skin
everlasting

spinning
in the smell

of a cigarette.

On A Windowsill In New York

Pigeons churn
their rooftop air-rights
like olive leaves turn
catching light.

                    At night
the streetlamp's amber arc
diffuses Bach's variations
to make starlight seem
twice as slow.

15

On steps
marrow-wet
searching a slash of light
under a siwash blanket
the hex enters the chest
with the applause of rain
on a windowpane.
                       Vivaldi
in stereo
but no Italian spring
muffled in a quilt.

16

Plugged,
the kitchen sink stinks.
Backed-up to the basement
by a wishbone maybe
washed away February
so the belly
sends up septic domes
no fizzling or plunging
could calm.
               The sludge
trailing on porcelain
each time the level subsides
likewise scores the skull

along the edge
of a mind's reservoir
dropping.

17

Oleo skids on a skillet;
the sun melts
thru a rip in the west;
winter rivets rust to flesh
& nothing's won in love
over a steamy mug
of lemon & honey,
gulps of Benylin
& the rattle of vitamins.

18

Pebbles in pavement,
anemones in neon,
put a foot on the curb
at the door of a pub.

The tablecloth releases
a length of thread
with a careful tug
while an undisturbed beer
anneals an amber thumb,
unable to purge
a week's weather.

19

Gallant these plants
crowded on a sill
to sprout in least light.

A day of non-event
aches by
glacially.

A crocus thrusts thru
an inch of snow;
a branch unlocks
a parade of petals
trembling.

21

At six
the taut tendons
of two contenders
gripped in a windy knot
over a chestnut tree
silhouetted on an oystershell.

22

Equinox.
Confusion menaces
seasons stuck
in a stasis of light.

Dormant thoughts
nudge darkly
like skull-spuds in burlap
barrowed to garden.

Two seats
(one each)
of two boards
one green
one grey
with a trace
of wine and green
on four stones
(two each)
where we eat
cucumber and munster
by scorched pine
sharp rock
above a traintrack
below an autoroute
a cafe of
two seats:
two boards
one sunbleached
mint green
one grey
with a trace
of rosé and
similar green
each on two stones:
host and hosted
lunar, alone.

Not exactly
rat a tat tat
or precisely
hissing
but
(you know Satchmo)
a continual
shifting locomotion:

Quasimodo's toes
tap gargoyles gargling
Bacardi
or Foyt's Ferrari
sidestepping
an oilslick
to full stop.

Plip. Plop.

        Drop-
loops
pass droploops;
moist bamboo
sprouts in saxophone soup
blue like lapis
smooth like catfur
like Mood Indigo

(no place to go
but up)

Mudpuddle
bubbledrums
pop Cassandra suds:
A Spanish sonata
for wet castanets.

Apparently
to read the signs
apples berries
bits of map

To unravel the strings
suspending the heart

travel a finger
over a Rosetta stone

and script what's written
in the glow
of the North Shore
from Kitsilano:

words minimally
struck in cuneiform.

Above that,
in daylight,
traces of snow
on indigo.

Three geese
equal
a chorus line:

they engage
time
with an eye
for audiences
too near
their stage.

Inaccessible
Zeigfield girls
they yield
to a handful
of seed.

Fresca rosa novella,
pious primavera,
by park, river
your red soprano
I declare rarest
among la verdura.

Your finesse finishes
heartless or beardless men
in celebration;
birds are agog
evening and morning
for such latin:
arbutus words.
(Caledonia! Cincinnati!
Incant Cavalcanti!
Angel-creator).

Angel semblance
reposes in you;
(God what adventure
fuels my destiny)!
Your clear gaze
a passing advance
on nature's costume,
a miracle's cause.
Indeed fra-lore
calls you goddess:
nothing contrary
adorns your presence;
you alone describe natura.

Human nature's altar

you face the face of God
Flora Regina,
Wildrose Alberta,
Sweetwine Granada;
(don't be rude
to a villain of providence).
And if I'm a herring,
an outrageous datepit,
don't blast me:
love alone forces it
without manners
or doubt.

The backdoor latch strains;
each hinge creaks
dry rust on rust;
within the week
gusts of grit in tourists' teeth
will say the season's over.

Eccentric dice trick
along the harbour;
a single skiff
sets to sea's labour.

Tavernas squawk
with summer stories;
old men watch
their beads and coffee.

Vespas putter empty streets;
shutters hang half open
on a north wind
fluttering the pounded silver sea,
steadily suspending curtain and skirt.

No need to stir
unless the earth quakes
and waiters stop chasing
tablecloths.

Barsponge, see-saw,
starless williwaw:

Berzerk dynamos;
helltongues carking,
gusts spinning.

Shadowlurk;
nothing to breathe
burnt in light.

Arctic empty
on the bottom step,
the cold shake.

Tightlipped spasms
in a collapse of mercury
on Eskimo Avenue
where one Marlboro pack
claps to the cuff
and the News
wraps a hydrant.

Hard gallantry it is amid
raw blades adrift
from boxcars of hacksaws
more maniac than shrapnel
fluttering the plastic over
ragheaps on steps.

No place to stand still
with chill decisions
crisscrossing every corner
and a compass gone screwy:

It's too cold to be alone.

Last week
the sky became solid rock
and only flocks of wild ducks
northern geese
relieved its weight.

This week
the leaves under the cherry tree
are like a catch of yellow fish
in a green sea.

Next week
rain will come incessantly
and the mountains will disappear.

These three October weeks
(drafts drifting over bathwater)
are the same every year
in Vancouver.

Abortion

In an afternoon
of skillsaws and crowcaws
she sleeps chilled.

　　　'She took my arm
　　　fragile pale
　　　wanting air'

Uncertain
birds watch cats
sun in sealaced air
puffing the curtain;
silent, distant
nausea aches
like cartires ache
pavement.

　　　'Driving there
　　　something circled
　　　unseen above
　　　reluctant wavering'

Released
she wakes;
winter creeps
up the mountain.

Speak of spurs
and faint footways
on an island peak
where you seek in stars and snow
the symmetry of bells and hands,
arrows and yellow berries.

Where snow-flowers on your sleeve
and bright night flowers
balance like tiny shrines
to god in your mind.

'The land is hard
but has vegetable love.
My waistband
like winterweed
sprouts to the ground
between seasons.'

I'll think of you
watching ants
carry breadcrumbs
from my cupboard
down the street
to their house:

a prolonging shadow
where the longest light
is in the corner of a meadow.

(The title refers to Johann Kepler's
A New Year's Gift Of Hexagonal Snow, 1611)

Mescal moon,
pearl button,
saddest light
I've ever seen
on fedora mountain:
                    Sierra Madre.

3 dead cows
by the highway.

A bright blanket
on a breeze.

Tequila:
the mind's limbo
beneath fanpalm.

I

Madness abounds where least expected;
warehouse and poolroom rebound
neglected logic.

            Some say
sadness hesitates advance;
others laugh at another chance.

Spun-out,
stripped of sense and nonsense,
flitting and floating on lithium and valium
like motes on a shaft of light,
we prefer our pardon:
vast equilibriums of tobacco and tea
without worry or delight;
Trieste or Toronto
have the same days
dribbling by
to nights safely asleep.

Who can blame us
or bare witness
left alone in life?

Whose skull
contains no stress
staring at emptiness?

     Scum dribbling
without spasm or blink
rings knots round
              cusp
of gullwing
        drumming
the bleak skin
over the East End.

Barnacles starfish suck
bracelet rock and timber
sunk in ochre
stroking brick
and rope
and waterweed
in mudfuzz flinching
from boot and bottle
on a bottom clam bubbles
and sand dollars claim.

Who could trust this chart
from flypost to gutter
to birdbath coloured
unreal rust?

To the left an inch
            and an inch more
to the right
        of green growing
between cathedral and Texaco,
diesel and nostril
           as we travel
scrounging scraps,
hiding the heart.

Who could have told
Heaven or Hell
standing still
in this hoof-hold?

The moon is gloom;
the stars are sterile.
Our despair vibrates in a vacuum
while bonescrapers tally
flesh from fat,
rats scatter to nest.

II

Up from the boats
blistering with thirst
I was touched for a butt
by silver gristle
and distilled candlewax
spinning through a blizzard:

'Believe me
there's no Chinese laundry
where the River Shannon flows...

Fate sucked my breath
in the prime of youth;
one boat between the blades
and the solar plexus shot
from my chest.
It was nothing to do with me:
I'd just as soon things

were like they were:
small, vacant, without despair.
Last night my best slacks
were boosted. Who cares?
You don't see me complaining;
I'm on vacation from everything;
my family and friends long gone.
I convalesce sort of melted,
unhinged; senseless in a justless maze
so intricately etched
I cringe to take up the thread,
unravel the web.
Besides, that was years ago.'

A man of small learning
leaned across the tabletop
nodding through the smoke;
the current of his slur
bent my ear:

'Believe me
utmost heat pardons none
sweating streaks across
memory's mirror steamed ashen;
swatting spirals thought puts up
like flies over waste of sand
and cactus blossom to hazed horizon.
I had no track to follow
or hope of progress groping lost,
parched as a desert ass,
throat too swollen to startle
buzzards from fallen flesh.

But some are lucky:
life is steady, unperturbed, casual;
events pass without event
natural as salmon unknowing.'

Jerking on the wind,
mumbling feebly,
always hoping
with sinking hope
this could be a dream,
styrofoam honeycombs
pop like pomegranate
shredded hysterical
on blacktop
dumb as death.

Shall we blame Saturn for Monday,
mad scabbed men with violins,
the dismal electric of High Holborn,
the stench of piss,
cracked pavement,
prices in general on a solar wind?

The river laps metallic;
night hangs on a tree's skeleton;
dread saps innocence
as if nothing mattered
but the scam of reason
defending a self's treason
accruing like leafmould
on language twisted
into a jeweller's chain
or the string restraining
balloons on a postcard rack.

Micro circuitries,
unreal galaxies,
flash heavenly graphics
in a credit column
crippled on a loop
of crackling nerves
while the fang of lizard lust
sip-sips the blush
of all our humility.

***

Went round to see Midas
one moonlit night
to better my teeth and worth.
Hordes at his doors and windows
craned bum and brain to his magic hand
but Midas of the Golden Touch,
Midas of the Easy Life
was discourteously transfixed.

'Out of sight
my fingers twitch,
chilled with the excitement
of my abacus singing,
calculating,
clicking back and forth.'

Wooden souls preserved in creosote
drove themselves like poles
around the molten flux;
others rose fungus lips
to mutter small complaint
until marshdawn unrolled
the sun on water
like a nugget of butter.

Wind whistling
billows
a hollow skin
scabbed to a skull —

There are no comforts
in Pompeii;
no days remorse
vacates the streets.

The sweep
    of the mountain,
the curve
    of heaven
dissolve
    to ash
and cloud patterns.

Nothing matters
or lasts longer
than a breath.
I recollect
the moons of Jupiter
gave us hope
the year Hermaphrodite
warned of withering:

August like a cradle,
    wind on wave's chevron;
lilacs on the leeside,
    lavender and mustard
to the horizon...

Stratagems in amber
      humans in light:

'a sad jar of atoms'

A confusion of goats
amid fumes uncoiling
dull as rope
from a pool melting
zero upon zero.

Compact:

We learn late
not enough
and blame life
too brief.

We cry light
relief
to slough
this weight.

Scoffed by us
what's lost
is cost
of all concern.

Acknowledgements

Some of these poems have appeared in *Literary Storefront Newsletter, Vers Sunyata,* and *Montemora.*